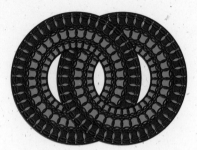

Where

the

Dead

Are

Where
the
Dead
Are

POEMS

Wanda S. Praisner

CavanKerry ◈ Press LTD.

CavanKerry Press Ltd.
Fort Lee, New Jersey
www.cavankerrypress.org

Library of Congress Cataloging-in-Publication Data

Praisner, Wanda S.
Where the dead are / Wanda S. Praisner. -- 1st ed.
p. cm.
Poems.
ISBN 978-1-933880-35-8 (alk. paper) -- ISBN 1-933880-35-X (alk. paper)
I. Title.

PS3616.R35W47 2013
811'.6--dc23

2012030943

Cover photo by Konstantinos Stampoulis
Cover and interior design by Gregory Smith
First Edition 2013, Printed in the United States of America

EMERGING VOICES
CavanKerry ❧ Press

CavanKerry Press is dedicated to springboarding the careers
of previously unpublished, early, and mid-career poets by
bringing to print two to three Emerging Voices annually.
Manuscripts are selected from open submission;
Cavankerry Press does not conduct competitions.

CavanKerry Press is grateful for the support it receives
from the New Jersey State Council on the Arts.

Contents

I

II

Coda

We don't know where the dead are.

But it's just as true, finally,

that we don't know where *we* are.

—Mark Doty

Where

the

Dead

Are

I

At the Exhibit

after Igor Svibilsky's photo "Fog 111"

I could enter the woodland scene. It seems
familiar, as though I'd been there before—
that sense of knowing, Lao Tzu spoke of,
that tints the soul, one life to another. But I'd be alone.
Come with me, you who welcomed me with a smile,
showed me where to go. Forget the lunch you were
preparing; I'll bypass the other rooms.
We'll step into the forest, its pale sepia fog,
journey together along the path—
a path I'll mention narrows in the distance.
You'll motion to two tree trunks arching high over us
to the other side, filigree branches feather-dusting
the ground. Air will be heavy with words we'll never say.
Here, now, you and I—no matter the way ahead's invisible.

Snow Globe

for S.J.P., 1967-1986

A mother and child enclosed,
sledding down a hill
that looks much like the one
outside my window—

green now with clover,
wild rose. Honeysuckle blooms,
no memory of January.
An orb of orange moon appears.

I stroke the glass,
shake and shake the sphere
until a snowstorm
hides the pair from view.

Wet and cold you kept on,
didn't want to come in.
After hot cocoa you asked,
"Is it my short
or long nap now?"
Short, I answered,
pulling down the shades.

Where the Dead Are

Backs to the sun, wings outstretched
anhinga-like, some two hundred vultures
sway in the stand of tulip trees
behind the school. More stork
than Old World vulture, they soar
on thermals. Shadows pattern the playground.
Children take no note of them.

Once upon a time I did.
Grossmutter on visits from Leonberg
would say they'd get me if I didn't clean
my plate. I ate to stay alive.
She'd return to Germany, leaving them in dark
corners of my room where the dead were.
It took nearly a lifetime to shoo them away.

Now the brazen black, not sated
with road kills and carcasses in the woods,
attack piglets, calves—eat asphalt shingles,
rubber roofing, leather upholstery.
I'm glad they're roosting out in the open
where I can count them each morning,
making sure all are where they should be.

Portrait of a Young Man

Lorenzo Lotto, c. 1530

I don't know why the pale sad face
attracts me or why the brown lizard
in the painting looks at him
from a shawl-covered table.

The staid curator says
such sadness was associated
with sensitive temperament

and the pamphlet explains
strewn rose petals
were a cure for melancholy.

The young man's back is turned
from a lute, a hunting horn,
a dead pheasant in the dark background.

A listless hand turns pages
in a book. The face, transfixed and white,
gazes out and down at nothing.
He could be dying—my son had such a pallor.

A Bereaved Parent Watches a Squirrel

Outstretched arms of the yucca
mound with snow. Among juncos
pecking the flake-speckled ground,
a squirrel raises front feet to white chest,
head back, looks up to the swaying
feeder filled with suet, thistle,
sunflower seed. As though demented,
it scurries up and down the cedar,
up and down the spruce, trying
to get where it needs to go,
its underground cache frozen.

It leaps, catches hold of the cord,
clings to the sleek and slippery dome
with teeth and claws until it reaches
the small openings—survival. No matter
that it loses balance, lands back
down again and again where it began—
somewhere in winter, when birds
can fall frozen from their branches—
somewhere in snowfall, above
buried bounty, below dangling lifeline.
It cannot do otherwise.

Reunion

I try to match the photo on the name tag with the woman
wearing it: round freckled face now drawn and lined,
long wavy red hair gone short, white. Drawing in on a
    Salem,
the way a child sucks through a straw, her lips curve
into a smile, setting the past straight, returning the girl
    everyone
envied forty years ago. She pages through the Reunion
    Book,
reads aloud her Fondest Memory, "Leading the Prom
    Procession."
In the restroom I ask about her husband, voted Best Athlete
in the yearbook. "He drank. We divorced. He's dead."

She takes me aside, lights up, puffs out a smoke screen.
"We had a child—a problem with anesthesia when she
    was two.
Lived to be twenty-two—blind, deaf. She died weighing
twenty-six pounds. It killed him." Her second husband
orders their fourth martini, followed by white zinfandels,
Irish creams—shows the tip he'll leave. At closing
    ceremonies
we're called up, the Cheerleaders—she, beside me,
    laughing
as we give a T-E-A-M, stir school spirit without benefit
of megaphones, uniforms, any observable heroes.

From the Ettersberg Memorial

Goethe's oak tree
on the Ettersberg
was spared when Buchenwald was built.

It stood between the kitchen
and the laundry—a stump now,
cemented in the center.

Goethe sketched alders and black poplar
along the Ilm. He painted
his stately city home

the same golden shade
as the maidenhair tree
he brought to Weimar—

SALVE, his usual greeting,
is lettered on the threshold.
In the cobblestone courtyard,
the carriage he used in town

and up the Ettersberg
where he spoke his maxim:
Let man be noble, helpful, and good.

From the crematorium
you can see the bear basin in the SS zoo
and Goethe's oak.

American generals made townspeople
climb the five steep miles
up the Ettersberg—

men with hats in hand,
women smiling, then
holding handkerchiefs to their faces.
We didn't know, they said.

From the memorial,
the sweep of countryside
takes your breath away.

Lewis Wickes Hine, Photographer
(1874-1940)

His 5,000 photographs helped end child labor.

Names for what they did:
Elsie, six, a *cartoner*
in a sardine factory; Minnie, nine,
a *cutter*, holds a knife
as long as her arm; Bessie, four,
an oyster *shucker*;

glass works *carrying-in-boys*;
tobacco *wormers, spikers,*
gatherers, stringers;
cotton mill *cone-winders, spoolers,*
spinners, doffers; Fred, three,
a *picker*: 20 pounds of cotton a day.

Box camera, dry-plate glass negatives,
Hine traveled to coal mines,
canneries, farms of every kind—
pale sepia testimony
to immigrant children
kept from school.

In a 1910 photo, Salvin,
a five-year-old in Browns Mills,
New Jersey, holds
two pecks of cranberries:
the bushel man pays a penny a pail;
"I don't never git no rest,"

a notation under a picture
of Henry, eight, a *beet-topper;*
a New York City *newsie,*
circa 1912, sleeps on his papers.
The magnesium flash
doesn't wake the seven-year-old.

From the Covered Bazaar

That afternoon it rained in Istanbul,
I rushed down side alleys lost
in silks, rugs, spices in burlap bags.
I emerged from that maze
into sudden saffron light
and you, waiting.
All else fell away as it did on seeing
the Topkapi's egg-sized emeralds,
the Dolmabahçe's crystal chandelier.

That night as we sipped milk-white raki,
you surprised me
with a spangled harem costume.
I gave you a glass evil eye.
Above the balcony an eyebrow moon arched
in a sky black as the Bosporus.
Lit minarets pointed starward.
Barefoot, I danced for you,
clicked finger cymbals,
while above the bed
the glass eye looked out,
held everything at bay.

Diving the Empress of Ireland

The *Titanic, Empress of Ireland,* and *Lusitania* were
all lost within three years of each other. The *Empress*
had the highest number of passenger fatalities.

Fingering a shining shard
my sons brought up from the silt
of the St. Lawrence,
I watch them unload empty tanks
and drysuits onto the driveway.
Only ten feet visibility, they say.
They toss out fragments of the story
as they hose down gear. Some died
outright on collision, blood
on the other ship's anchor points—
some awakened to last seconds
before inhaling frigid water—
a few escaped through portholes
as she rolled to starboard—
others jumped into a starless
fogbound night.
Fourteen minutes to sink.
I'm glad you're home, I say—
wonder if they think
of their brother drowned
in a safe place,
doing a safe thing.
*We didn't go see the skull
in the lifeboat,* they say.
I picture the jardiniere whole

as I trace the shard's
sharp edges, its raised
and gilt design,
violet and peach flowers
all under an overglaze
with no age lines.

My Eighth Grade Graduation Dress

Because Mother didn't drive,
Barbara Largo's mom took us
to Sussman's in Port Richmond
for patterns and fabric—
the same dress for all the girls:
square ruffled neck, cap sleeves,
peplum skirt, white cotton eyelet.

Because Mother didn't sew,
Mrs. Turberville, in the apartment
below, helped me on Saturdays

to pin down tissue,
cut with pinking shears, match notches,
sew pieces together.

From Mrs. Turberville's window
I could see Mother's monthly rags
flapping on the upstairs line.

Rust stains, she called them,
ignoring family complaints—
the real shame that now
mine hung there too.

Yesterday, as I changed
Mother's Depends—making sure
to wrap away the soiled one
so she wouldn't try to wash it—

she said, *You're mistaken,*
I haven't menstruated in years.
I don't need padding anymore.

Toward the City

But the stars burn on overhead,
Unconscious of final ends
—W. H. Auden

Driving the Turnpike, you do not look
toward a skyline violated,
turn instead to the sun

lowering in coral glory. It seems to pause
on the horizon, homage-like.
It backlights the jets lined up.

Past Newark you see planes aloft
and remember the hundreds grounded
in the Mojave, shined for better days—

fuel drained, cabins sealed like tombs.
You exit, cross Goethals to the island.
Dusk descends like a pall, overspreads,

deepens. First lights, shades of nephrite
and carnelian—the Verrazano,
strands of turquoise linking boroughs.

Soon stars move in what could be
a Nubian sky. The return home
past what was taken.

The Barefoot Contessa

Ava Gardner Museum, Smithfield, North Carolina

Fame brought me nothing I would have wanted.

As a girl she walked barefoot
in tobacco fields, liked the give of mud
between her toes, disliked shoes,
left them in mailboxes while visiting friends.
Another beauty beat her out as high school
    queen.

A lone magnolia's the backdrop at her grave,
still covered in pink roses. It's raining
like in the opening of *The Barefoot Contessa*.
Nearby in her museum, huge photos,
lips full and aflame as the crepe myrtle in bloom.

A documentary highlights
her golden moments on the silver screen—
my favorites: *Show Boat*, and *The Night of the Iguana*.
A close up taken by a relative started it all.
I always felt like a prisoner of my own image, she said.

This backwater town's lone magnolia
transplanted to the boulevards of the world.
She died abroad—a stroke, pneumonia.
As promised, Gregory Peck took in
her housekeeper and Welsh corgi at the end.
Framed pictures of her many visits home.

"She was a virgin when she married Rooney,
and never needed any of Sinatra's money,"
sharply comments a tour guide who knew her.
"Artie Shaw mocked her lack of education."

On display, the khaki jacket
worn in *Mogambo*, about the time
she aborted Sinatra's baby.
The rose-pink silk dress from Howard Hughes
when silk was reserved for parachutes.

Opera glasses, rings, gloves, purses.
A pair of gold-strap high heels—
small dark bits of matted dust and perspiration
on the leather innersoles
where her bare feet had been.

Anchored Off Korkula, Croatia

I close my eyes to see if I can hold
this moment, endure its absence.
Tomorrow we raise anchor.
Our time here is brief.

Dark cypress against a pink oleander sky.
A rose moon rises
behind the town fortress, church tower,

forms a water path
toward the ship where I sit
listening to stars come out.

Evening island sounds—
melancholy Croatian singing, a dog barking.
A bell tolls the death of another hour

and thoughts of my child return.
On a night blacker than this,
he went away and never came back.

His face emerges from the dark;
no need for lighted candles.
Unbidden, the past arrives,
sits so close I can feel its breath.

Intrusion

This man in green scrubs
snakes his way inside my heart,
chats as he clicks, notices
my toes fluttering up and down,
says my stents are ok,
no new blockages.

Through breezy corridors,
one wing to another,
I'm wheeled back to my room
and you, waiting—
once the only one
allowed into my heart.

Death at Ballyhoo's

Forget that hooded cloak & darkness crap.
I've got a job to do, & do it well. I'm everywhere.
I'm next to you right now at the bar in Ballyhoo's
& you don't even recognize me
as you motion for another brew—
me with G & D sunglasses crowning
my dark wavy hair, despite a dusting of snow
on the beach across the street. I'm ordering
a very dry Gray Goose martini for myself—
up, with a twist—a cosmo for the blonde
chick I've just met. She's into my liquid, bottomless
eyes, digs the black leather, flat abs, white shirt
opened to the belt—has already forgotten the forecast
for late night black ice on the roads.

Son, Your Belongings

Space now for visiting grandchildren,
told of your one-dimpled smile,
thumbs and knees that bent backwards.

A room you expected to return to
emptied: furniture, books, clothes—
a room it took years for us to enter.

One last pile remains centered
on the new carpet—the momentum lost:
a plastic Sheraton ice bucket you took
because the "S" stood for your name;

your Polaroid, strap broken;
a pair of Nikes, split at the soles;
college notebooks—
the last date: September 15, 1986.

What your brothers call "trash,"
what they don't want, I return
white-boxed like a casket to your closet—
even the sneakers, still laced.

Amanyara: "Peaceful Place"

Providenciales, the Turks and Caicos, October 2006

Pillow-propped on a lounge
outside the villa, a woman reads
a Stephen Dobyns's poem, is struck by the words:
"the radio describes the wounded day"

Inside, the man turns on the news—
Yankees pitcher and flight instructor
dead after small plane crash
into East River high-rise.

She wonders why he's allowed the world
entry into their Eden—is about to turn off the TV
when a Bahamian mockingbird
strikes the wall of glass, drops.

Yesterday, a gray gnatcatcher
slammed into the same place; the day before,
a perula warbler lay stunned
on its back for an hour.

The couple decides against another vigil—
she to the beach, he, the pool.
On their return the mockingbird's gone.
He samples fresh fruit, chilled champagne.

She touches a small gray feather
stuck to the pane—the reflected garden
real enough for any creature to see
the way ahead is clear. No fog, no barrier,

no brick wall to bring the airborne down.
The lucky open their eyes, flutter wings, flip over—
hop a bit before lifting up again
into their worlds, the scantling days.

Along the Trail

A child's red rubber ball
and an empty water bottle tumble,
caught under a yard-high waterfall
in the North Branch of the Raritan,
and thoughts return, son,

how you left without my having felt
your final warmth—
a life kept inside me,
safe in womb water

until it was time to separate—
you to breathe on your own.
You scored a perfect 10
on the Apgar scale.

Pool water your last inhale,
lungs filled, body cooled to cold
and blue rigidity as you sank
into another kind of water world—
only I wasn't there.

I wasn't there the next morning
when they found you on the bottom
and brought you out—the mouth
I never kissed goodbye,
covered in bloody froth—

I now left, as Rilke wrote,
*in the startled space
which a youth as lovely as a god
had suddenly left forever*

Over and over, again and again,
the ball and bottle circle, tossed
against the curtain of water, trapped
in foam, the ongoing turmoil.

Pythian Sibyl

The hands and arms are modeled
from my own, the sculptress
told Garnier, who commissioned
a bronze *Pythian Sibyl*
for his Paris Opéra
to be placed in a grotto
under the great staircase.

Reptiles seethe in her hair,
lizards writhe up from the pool,
green water casts an up-light
on the twisting figures.
She is all movement,
the body all tension—
the knit brow, open mouth.

Cross-legged on a pedestal
she leans forward,
her right arm braced behind,
the left outstretched to the side,
fingers spread, as if warding off evil,
her head turned toward a dread
she alone can see.

Later in the news
a continent away,
I see what the seer foresaw:
a runaway girl, raped
and mutilated, left for dead.
She holds up the remains of her arms
to slow the loss of blood.

Son,

I thought I saw you in a crowd.
I searched for your face,
but knew it couldn't be you—
drowned in your college pool.

I searched for your face—
the smile, the angle of jaw—but
you drowned in the lap pool,
left overnight.

The smile, angle of jaw—
my grief a cello.
You, left overnight,
lifeguards locked up—

the sound of a cello
replacing what is gone.
Lifeguards locked up—
if only they'd looked—

and then you were gone.
But I knew it couldn't be you.
If only they'd looked.
I thought I saw you in a crowd.

II

Aboard the Tigress

the Galapagos, 1980

We bathed in the sea
those weeks on the schooner,
only liquid Joy worked up a lather.

The English biologist pointed out
killer whales, a Portuguese man-of-war,
showed where the spiny lobster hid.

The Ecuadorean mate deep-fried thick
fritters and French toast for our sons—
three of them then.

One later drowned in his college pool.

When the sun dropped straight below
the horizon at six o'clock, without
a twilight, only a green flash,

we'd go to bed, watch
the Southern Cross
in the hatch above our bunks,

the German captain radioing back
to Santa Cruz, *Alles in Ordnung*—
everything in order, and so it was.

Come Night

She watches beetles eat
through the backyard garden.
She really should weed the beds.
Once, she would have crushed each insect
neatly between two petals.

She thinks of the night before,
the meeting room she entered for the first
time, strangers seated in a circle
she forced herself to name *my new family.*
"Only we understand," they said.

She listened to each story,
told how her child died,
thought grief must be like the hot tea she held—
a matter of letting it go cold in the cup,
a matter of waiting.

She looks up to the line of windows
under the shingled roof. Come night,
she thinks, in bituminous dark—
all the bedroom lights will be on but his.

Mummy at El Plomo: An Offering

Who readied the eight-year-old
for the climb up the Chilean Andes—
his face reddened as a sign
of life, lines like sunlight
radiating to the cheeks;
long hair oiled and plaited
into more than
two hundred braids;
a tuft of condor feathers
on the headdress of human hair;
the wide silver bracelet and pendant;
a cloak of alpaca wool.

Who chose what would be
entombed with him—
the pouches of baby teeth,
fingernail clippings, matted hair;
two small llamas:
one of hammered and soldered
gold, silver, copper,
the other of Spondylus shell;
a silver female figurine
in miniature dress,
coral parrot feathers
arching from the cap.

Who walked him to his grave
of permafrost and stones—
almost 18,000 feet—
his feet swollen and numb
in thinnest moccasins;
vomit on his tunic from
the corn beer or coca leaves
to ease the end—
by nightfall
the sacrifice to Inca
Sun or Water god complete,
child deified,
family honored.

Was his mother among those
who praising the gods
turned away and left him
huddled into himself,
head tilted, resting on raised
knees, arms encircling—
a countenance so life-like,
that even after
five hundred years
it seems a touch or word
could wake him,
tell him it is time
to go home.

In the KZ Mauthausen Museum

Vorwärts,
      unsere Leitung
      Freiheit oder Tod

The glass display case
holds examples of prisoners'
Handarbeit, handwork
not much different
from the arts and crafts
you'd see in a store window
on the Hauptstrasse in Linz.

Only these are smaller—
more like end-of-day pieces
artisans created
from what was left
after the labor was done—
the self, expressed,
something their own:

a salamander, key, a dog
carved from bone;
a pair of mittens woven
from random colored threads;
a fabric purse closed
with a single snap—
all less than an inch long.

But I'm drawn
to a two-inch heart-shaped
notepad, covered in cloth—-
a string at each pointed end
to tie and close for privacy.
On the opened page in script
an eighth of an inch high:

> *Onward,*
> *our direction*
> *freedom or death*

> —*Lisa*

New York City Sandhog:
The Third Water Tunnel, 1997

Work begun in 1970, to be completed in 2020

Like medieval stonemasons laboring
on a grand cathedral, the work of the father's
the work of the son—
everyone here's the son or nephew
of a sandhog. Irish, West Indians.

Nicknames passed down
like a prized gold watch—some modified
over time: Buster begot Chipper; Hard Rock
became Soft Rock; Ace, Deuce.

Still the most dangerous work,
despite machines to replace explosives,
hand tools, and horses.
Eighty stories of rock above,
rock four hundred million years old
objecting to intrusion—

being where no one's been—
the need for kinship, bonding,
sandhog to sandhog.
Tunneling, Westchester to the four boroughs,
will span a human lifetime.

Boots on, earplugs in,
bundled in flannel, wool, a yellow
jumpsuit and slicker, the descent
eight hundred feet in a metal cage—
connecting shafts and valve chambers
the size of zeppelin hangers—

a pearly haze, air poisonous with fumes,
silica dust that penetrates
filters on respirators—
noise enough to rupture eardrums.

No one lingers under a shaft: falling
rock, ice, tools, lunch pails—a cigarette lighter
can go through a sandhog,
head to foot, hard hat or not.

Down the line till the conduit's done,
cemented over, shaft covered, maybe
a parking lot or small park above.
A billion gallons a day will scream
through the new tunnel

and no one will be here again.
It's why it's mapped, notes taken,
so engineers not yet born
will know the faulting.

For now, knee-deep muck to slog through,
dripping walls, weak rock banded to sound,
a ceiling studded with bolts
to ward off a cave-in,
metal stretchers with body bags
propped against the wall—

Smitty, from Granada, the latest—
his real name, Thomas Noel.
Always a smile, nothing got to him.
His leg ripped off. Cardiac arrest.
Hauled a mile, tunnel to shaft.
The mayor came to his wake.

A life for every mile
already ahead of schedule;
twenty miles, twenty-four dead—
only yesterday, another. Forty to go.

Last Night in Singapore

I don't know exactly what a prayer is.
I do know how to pay attention.
— Mary Oliver

Twenty stories above the city
a low cloud stalls
over the rooftop pool,
white as the sickle moon—
explosions of spider lilies
from darkened foliage.

In the room, CNNI news
of a TWA crash in New York—
pictures of luggage hauled
from Long Island waters
looking much like my bags
packed and ready at the door.

Midnight at Changi Airport—
last minute buying:
batik and jade,
boxes of Joaquim orchids.
Stewardesses in sarongs
hurry to check in—

my pulse rate rising
on the short walk
across marble floors
to the gate, the waiting 747—
the high clouds,
the same white moon.

Plea

You pleaded, even quoted
Shakespeare's "Lady,
shall I lie in your lap?"
But I denied you, erected
a high wall to separate
love from desire. Now I am left
with a tin badge, a body
I should have given—
you now gone from yours—
and I wonder how I ever thought
the two could be divided, and why
I withheld the half that doesn't last.

Detour in Connecticut

He abruptly turns off Route 5,
pulls over and leaves the car—
I've had enough!—

Afternoon freezes into evening,
she waits, still as snow
in a night of silence and white

knowing he'll return to set her straight
before getting back in the right direction—

northeast. There, as usual,
like the tree and window lights,

he'll outshine everyone with trivia,
a string of anecdotes.

She sees herself drive off
alone, back to a warmer climate,
back to her garden—

paths below melon oleander,
lemon yellow hibiscus

where the lizard, unlike the chameleon,
keeps to its own color.

New snow falls, wind weaves a white veil
against the panes.

A rush of cold at the sight of him
opening the door.

Woman in Black

Entering the water,
you raise a bangled veil,
place a mask against your face,

bend to pull on fins,
silk abaaya a second skin
as you fall forward into the Red Sea.

In your first abaaya
gifted after the awaited menses,

as a child, torn from bed,
spread open on a mat,
did you stumble in a world gone dim?—

the arranged marriage, the halawa—
a paste of red-hot rose water, sugar
and lemon juice to rid the body of hair.

Breathing through the tube
you stroke right, kick toward the horizon.

Being There: September '01

for W.S. and D.W

The afternoon my mother died,
a crowd at the firehouse near the theatre—
Engine 54, Ladder 4. Above the door:
NEVER MISSED A PERFORMANCE.
Photos of the captain and his company—
red, white, and blue sidewalk candles,

donated cakes, a book to sign,
children's drawings of the Towers.
In one, stick figures midair,
hair flying, bodies curved,
a dog plummeting too—
on the afternoon my mother died.

I saw the play *The Producers*
the afternoon my mother died,
September nineteenth—
she in the hospital that week.
"Only a few days," her doctor said.
I said I'd see her in the evening.

Nathan Lane had a day off,
the afternoon my mother died.
The captain, my cousin's husband,
lost with his men inside the Marriott.
"He shouldn't have been there,"
my cousin said. "It really was his day off."

In Johannesburg: 2002

Saturday nights, the hostel hall packed.
Men in purple suits, velvet vests
and polka-dot ties
vie for best-dressed award,
a prize of six dollars.
No matter barbed wire and bullets outside.
Inside, there's style.

Without music or spotlight
gentlemen strut across a cement floor—
pants creased blade-sharp,
wingtips polished.
A smooth shuffle, a slow spin,
tip of a fedora—
smiles lingering
long after the applause.

I feel important here, says Piet Zulu
who on weekdays mixes cement.
When I walk, I walk tall.
On special days like Christmas,
the winner is given a live goat.
Whenever I'm in a suit
I tell myself I'm beautiful.

Visiting Higher Bockhampton Cottage

This house Thomas Hardy returned to—
thatch roof, cob walls, chamfered beams—
his sketch of Wessex in the hall:
Dorset's heathland, coastline,
great chalk downs, lanes snaking
hamlet to hamlet, farm to farm.
Upstairs the room where at birth
he was *thrown aside as dead*
till the nurse called out,
"Stop a minute; he's alive enough, sure!"—
where his mother found him asleep
in his cradle, a snake come in
with the furze, curled on his chest. I sit
in the window seat where he looked out
to gorse-covered Blackdown Hill,
its monument to his hero,
Admiral Thomas Hardy; I step carefully
down ladder stairs to the kitchen
where he made cider with his grandmother.
The smell of milk pudding cooked overnight
in the firebrick oven, cooling and setting
like the tales of rural folk she told—
his imagination kindled, sparks flamed
into Jude, Tess, Bathsheba.

This garden he returned to—
walls overrun with sweet pea, japonica,
beds of lupines and lavender
where he'd find himself

without a scrap of paper
at the very moment he felt volumes
the need to resort to leaves, woodchips,
pieces of stone or slate that came to hand.
This garden he still saw, spoke of
when days of visiting ended.
As I leave, I take photos
of red admirals and peacock butterflies
signing among bluebells and foxgloves,
entering to take what is needed
before moving on.

Delos

for my father

No one's born or buried here.
Scientists dig, Greeks supervise,
tourists visit. Guides describe
a mosaic floor on a museum wall:
"Athena in a helmet—masks decorate
the border." One intact and realistic face
smiles out, haunts me—but how to recall a past
I cannot reconstruct.

Fig trees rise from empty cisterns,
stairs lead down to a fountain
green with algae and croaking frogs.
Once, ten thousand slaves changed hands
daily in the agora. The sacred lake drained
for fear of malaria, overgrown with tamarind.
A tall palm marks the site where Apollo was born
to shiver in island wind.

Purple, parchment-like statice covers hillsides.
I pick a sprig, pocket a white stone
and suddenly realize you'd been here,
fifty years ago, and done the same—
later asking me to print *DELOS, 600 BC*
on your souvenir, glue on the purple flower.
I did. I'd forgotten.
You, unearthed—we, for a moment, restored.

Gillam Bay, the Bahamas: June 2004

I'm a mile out in Gillam Bay collecting sand dollars, tellins,
and cockleshells, and suddenly there's no bottom to stand on.
This is how the Chinese cockle-pickers must have felt
stranded out in England's Morecambe Bay last February:
tide coming in like a freight train as they dug on mud flats,
filling buckets; panic, struggling to stay afloat;
exhaustion, acceptance, letting go.

I tread water, calm down, tell myself I can swim
against the current keeping me from shore.
I gain control and make it back.
Guo Binglong's last call on his cell phone to his wife
5,000 miles away: "I am up to my chest in water.
Maybe I am going to die." The drowned identified
by watches and wallets, their photos and good-luck
    charms.

Pausing for Tony Blair
in the Forbidden City

Please to watch high thresholds we step over
in Forbidden City, ya. My English name, Charlie, ya,
Charlie. Rooms here, many, go on and on
like dynasties, ya. Notice bed of emperor
in room at right, royal seals in room at left.
We meet outside. Ten minutes, ya, ten minutes.

Now we wait in shade, ya, a delay,
Tony Blair here. So I tell how dynasty keep on,
ya, I tell you this. At night when mandarins
and other royal relatives leave, emperor only
male left inside walls, ya,—120 empresses
and concubines for him, ya, for him.

You know yang? Ya, male force—not so strong
like ying, ya, female force—so emperor
need much ying to build up enough yang
to father son of Heaven, ya, son of Heaven.
So he have sex with concubines with no climax—
ya, orgasm, ya—ha, ha—he store up lots of yang

for monthly visit with esteemed empress, ya, wife.
Names of royal wives and favorites
on jade tablets by emperor chamber, ya,
outside bedchamber. He turn over name of one
he want each night, eunuch on duty
rush to find lucky lady.

She wear no clothes, so no weapon hidden.
Foot-bound little lady wrapped in yellow cloth
and carried on back—how you say? ya, piggy-back,
to royal bedroom—put at feet of emperor, ya, at feet.
Eunuch write name, date, and time
to check in case of child, ya, in case of baby.
So, dynasty go on. Ya. Now we go on.
Please to watch high thresholds we step over.

Today

a sound is heard, strokes of the axe
—Anton Chekhov, *The Cherry Orchard*

Across the way, new owners
alter my parents' house: added garages,
a second basement, more rooms—
a hole in the earth, a mound of soil—

yesterday accommodating tomorrow.
Their cherry trees are down.

I look away, turn to the paper:
June Allyson died—
sunny, raspy-voiced movie star
married to Dick Powell.

Mom liked him even better
than Rudy Vallee or Bing Crosby.

American GIs in the 1940s pinned up
photos of Betty Grable and Rita Hayworth,
but it was June Allyson—Dad's favorite—
they wanted to come home to.

And news today: real estate agents tour
the late Aaron Spelling's 1980s mansion,
built on Bing Crosby's former estate.
Always the sound of the axe in the orchard.

Bora Bora

She can't stop filming a pair
of orange angelfish circling
a coral head. His words echo:
I want out! We're two strangers
living under the same roof!

She exits the water—a pair
of fairy terns fly 'round and 'round
a cordia tree by their bungalow.
Orange flowers litter the deck.

He's back at the dock snapping
schools of mullets, Mount Otemanu
in the background, its peak
crowned with clouds like a headdress
of white plumeria blooms.

Blades on the bedroom ceiling fan
blur, become the circle.
She takes off her gold wedding band,
places it on his nightstand.

Silence on the way home,
only the drone of propellers.
Below, an orange sunset on an atoll,
constellations of *motu* islets
in a universe of sea.

One last picture in the fading light:
a crescent of over-water bungalows
gracing the smooth lagoon
like a native shell necklace.

In need of two hands to clasp it shut,
she thinks, putting away her camera—
noticing a white band
where her ring had been.

An Unaccustomed Clasp

How effortlessly
my fingers meet,
slide past,
fall down enfolded
in an embrace.
A folding of hands,
a moment for thanks,
for help.
For long,
an unaccustomed clasp.
Forgive.

Overcast October First

A friend called from the UK,
wished me Happy Rabbit's Day, luck
for the first of the month, a family custom.
Here too it's fog, no luck finding
the great blue heron, actually gray, absent
since leaves began to fall. Like time,
when you look for it, it's never there—
September and all its losses gone—
I cut short my son's last call to watch TV,
told my mother in the hospital
I'd visit in the evening—
the silence now of words never spoken.

My friend ended the call
with Happy White Rabbit's Day
what his granddaughter wished him earlier,
but I'm still with gray: the rabbit's foot
my grandfather gave me after butchering one
for supper, I not knowing what luck was,
still don't. But I know gray: squirrels
crossing the meadow, nuts carried
in mouths for burial; a rabbit foot matted
in blood; the heron spending time elsewhere,
gone without a goodbye—
no well-wishes, not even See you later.

Invitation

winter 1986

Once I avoided thoughts of Death
to keep him from my life,
pictured him dark-eyed, dark-haired,
a cunning plunderer between jobs,

sharpening his scythe in a backroom
somewhere, but he came,
found my son swimming
in his college pool and took him.

Now I tempt his return by driving
icy roads over the Bernardsville Hills
instead of using Route 202,
salted and sanded. But he's busy
elsewhere, inventing guises.

My son's face and smile begin to fade—
why Rembrandt painted his wife
as the funeral bells tolled,
while he still could see her,

stroking her in brocade, rubies
around her white throat—before
she would be lost and beyond him
as her body in the grave.
Come, the door's open, the light's out.

A Run before Sleep

A pumpkin moon looms
behind black locust trees—

above, a speckle of stars—
night drawing attention to itself.

A black dog suddenly at my side
keeps silent cadence
until I pass.

So many houses owned
by the young again—

those who lived in them
float ghost-like beside me,
voices echo with my footfalls.

I forget how many times
I pass the NO OUTLET sign,

think instead of this morning—
a child in church

clutching the air, trying
to catch particles of dust.

Coda

Making Egg Salad

It's not easy to remove shells
from hard-boiled eggs—the sink
layered with bits of white, chips
of pink, yellow, blue, and green,
purple too, your favorite color.

Yesterday in church the priest said,
Oh, how nice you're all here today!
But we weren't. You were missing.
He may have regretted his words—
if he'd remembered.

Nineteen years since you left us
in your nineteenth year.
Such a great fall, all the king's horses,
all the king's men long gone—

we're still in pieces. Like now—
discovering that a crack on the top
will separate membrane and shell
from the womb-shaped body.

Reaching for the Stars

As a child, in bed with rheumatic fever,
I sent to Hollywood for autographed
glossies that crossed the continent
to 86 Sheridan Avenue—
celestial beings come down to earth
on Staten Island, 1943, to be with me—

collected into a scrapbook,
later lost when we moved—
that long year when I couldn't go along
to Stapleton's Liberty Theater
for the latest movie, the cup or saucer
mother collected toward her set of dishes.

Now I flip through black and white photos
of old film stars in Provincetown's
Remembrance of Things Past,
a shop on Commercial Street—
some screen greats like Garbo
and Bogart become legends—

and I can't resist close-ups of Carole Lombard,
Barbara Stanwyck, and Veronica Lake,
can't wait to be handed my bag filled with stars
as I picture mother coming up the stairs,
bringing Ovaltine in her new cup and saucer,
saying, *A package came for you today.*

Jungfrau: Evening

Wengen, 2000

Clouds cross eastward over snowfields.
Shadows on mountain evergreens
deepen like regret.
Seven o'clock and chimney swifts
begin to cheep and circle the depot clock,
sweep so close they sway geraniums
blooming on the balcony.
Once my young son and I hiked here—
he at rest now in the earth. Today I can
hardly climb onto the cog railway car.

Without my watching, the sun
lowers. The ticking and sweeps keep on.
At nine the last train waits in the station.
Too cool to stay out any longer.
First lights visible far below
in distant Lauterbrunnen.
Birds settle under overhangs.
I can still make out the clock,
hands motionless,
almost at a standstill.

Momma in the Heavens

Above your new grave, a jet lowers
for its final approach into Newark,
and I hear your words from fifty years ago:
"I won't go." But you did,

unable to deny me my first flight
to visit my German grandmother.
You must have been praying
as you sat in veiled hat and white gloves,
not eating or drinking. You refused

to look out, Daddy making it worse
when he tried to reassure you
the plane could still fly on two motors
if the other propellers failed.

To camouflage the smell of cigarette smoke,
a stewardess sprayed Elizabeth Arden's
Blue Grass through the cabin
and up toward the empty storage shelf.

During the night, a whispering, aisle to aisle:
We've reached the point of no return.
Daddy explained it was now longer
to turn around and go back,
that we had to keep on, no matter what.

Your gloved hand in mine,
I parted the window curtain to look for stars—
nothing but a sparkplug
separating us from the dark.

For Sothy, Angkor Guide:
Siem Reap, Cambodia

September 2005

For your dark eyes
in which I did not read "tourist."

For your villagers, bones and skulls
found in killing fields
displayed in a roadside stupa.

For the babies tossed in air
to land on a carpet of nails.
Rouge means red, you said.

For Pancourt, your grandmother,
burned alive naked,
buried in a common grave.

For your mother, who found
your grandmother's red shirt.

For you, a child of eight,
tied to a tamarind tree, then
covered with red ants.

For your body
turned red with welts,
your head swelled.

For Vishnu, the protective god
　　you invoked to inspire me.

For your picture, given to me
　　as we parted. Your last words:
　　How good to be alive, yes?

A Gift

On hands and knees I closet-dig
for my Edna St. Vincent Millay book
to find her sonnet that begins:

"Well, I have lost you"—possibly
stacked on the floor, buried behind
an old lamp I may need someday.

Dust motes rise as I move aside
outdated shoes, flush out boxes—
the way my basset uncovers a bone.

No book, but I remove a pair of pumps
in style again, and the lamp,
shove the rest back—except for a folder

labeled School Photos. Inside,
my son's eighth-grade graduation picture.
Six years later we placed him

into the earth. I remember the end:
"Should I outlive this anguish—and men do—
I shall have only good to say of you."

Acknowledgments

I am grateful to the following journals for publishing my poems:

Atlanta Review: "For Sothy, Angkor Guide: Siem Reap, Cambodia," "Mummy at El Plomo: An Offering," "New York City Sandhog: The Third Water Tunnel, 1997"

Edison Literary Review: "Aboard the *Tigress*"

Gathered on the Mountain: "From the Covered Bazaar," "Last Night in Singapore," "Woman in Black"

Journal of New Jersey Poets: "A Gift," "Diving the *Empress of Ireland*," "From the Ettersberg Memorial," "Making Egg Salad," "Reunion"

Kelsey Review: "Delos," "Invitation"

Lutheran Women: "An Unaccustomed Clasp"

Main Street Rag: "Jungfrau: Evening"

MARGIE: "In Johannesburg: 2002," "Lewis Wickes Hine, Photo-grapher (1874-1940)," "*The Barefoot Contessa*"

Paterson Literary Review: "Momma in the Heavens," "Where the Dead Are," "Reaching for the Stars"

Prairie Schooner: "Overcast October First"

Slant: "Amanyara: "Peaceful Place," "Today"
Up and Under: the QND Review: "Gillam Bay, the Bahamas: June 2004"

US 1 Worksheets: "A Run Before Sleep," "Death at Ballyhoo's," "De-tour in Connecticut," "Intrusion," "Portrait of a Young Man," "Snow Globe"

"Momma in the Heavens," "Reaching for the Stars," and "Where the Dead Are" were honorable mentions in the *Paterson Literary Review*'s Allen Ginsberg Awards. "For Sothy, Angkor Guide: Siem Reap, Cambodia," "Mummy at El Plomo: An Offering," and "New York City Sandhog: The Third Water Tunnel, 1997" were honorable mentions in the *Atlanta Review*'s International Competitions. "Mummy at El Plomo: An Offering" was included in the *Atlanta Review*'s 10th Year Anthology. "At the Exhibit" was a winner in the D & H Greenway Princeton Land Trust Contest: "The Road Not Taken." "Delos," "Diving the *Empress of Ireland*," and "Snow Globe" were nominated for the Pushcart Prize. "From the Ettersberg Memorial," "Pythian Sibyl," and "Snow Globe" won First Prize in Poetry (judged by Denise Duhamel, Paul Muldoon, and Yusef Komunyakaa) at the College of New Jersey Writers' Conference. "In Johannesburg: 2002" was a finalist in the 2004 *MARGIE* "Strong Rx Medicine" Contest, selected by Thomas Lux. "Where the Dead Are" appeared in my chapbook *On the Bittersweet Avenues of Pomona* (Spire Press Award Winner, 2006).

I thank the Artist/Teacher Institute, US 1 Poets' Cooperative, South Mountain Poets, Peter Murphy's Getaways, and The Frost Place where many of these poems were read and critiqued, as well as the New Jersey State Council on the Arts for its 1995-96

Poetry Fellowship and the Geraldine R. Dodge Foundation for several fellowships to the Provincetown Fine Arts Work Center and the Virginia Center for the Creative Arts. I am grateful to Renée Ashley, Robert Carnevale, Thomas Dooley, Mark Doty, Sondra Gash, Maria Mazziotti Gillan, Joan Cusack Handler, Jean Hollander, Molly Peacock, Thomas Praisner, Jane Rawlings, Nancy Scott, and Elizabeth Anne Socolow for their help and guidance. My warmest thanks to Baron Wormser for his vision and patience.

Finally, I want to thank my teachers, Sr. Anne Ford and Stephen Dunn for their early and continued encouragement, kindness, and inspiration; and to my ever-supportive family, especially my husband, Bob.

Other Books by Wanda S. Praisner

A Fine and Bitter Snow (2003)

On the Bittersweet Avenues of Pomona (2006)

CavanKerry's Mission

Through publishing and programming,
CavanKerry Press connects communities of
writers with communities of readers. We publish
poetry that reaches from the page to include
the reader, by the finest new and established
contemporary writers. Our programming brings
our books and our poets to people where they
live, cultivating new audiences and nourishing
established ones.

Other Books in the Emerging Voices Series

CavanKerry now uses only recycled paper in its book production. Printing this book on 30% PCW and FSC certified paper saved 2 trees, 1 million BTUs of energy, 127 lbs. of CO_2, 67 lbs. of solid waste, and 524 gallons of water.